WORLD WAR 2

Stories of the Schutzstaffel:
True Accounts of Hitler's Personal
Bodyguards

Cyrus J. Zachary

LIKE BOOKS?

Would you like them delivered to you every week?

Do you like non-fiction books on a huge range of different topics?

We send out e-books every week so we can share our books with the world!

We have books every week on AMAZON that we send to our email list.

So if you want in, then visit the link at the end of this book to sign up and sit back and wait for new books to be sent straight to your inbox!

TABLE OF CONTENTS

Introduction

Chapter 1

Chapter 2

Chapter 3

Chapter 4

Chapter 5

Conclusion

INTRODUCTION

The world has seen some very nasty men throughout the centuries of human civilization and one of the worst of the lot was Adolf Hitler of Germany.

The instigator and the mastermind behind the Holocaust, the man was at the forefront of the Second World War and ruined millions of lives, throwing the entire European continent into chaos. Not only was he hated by the whole world, even some of his own military commanders didn't like him.

And yet, in the many years that he ran his tight regime, not one assassination attempt was successful. Hitler, in the end, died by his own hand – when it became obvious that Germany was going to lose the War, he killed himself, refusing to submit to the Allied Powers.

Any and all attempts to kill him on the part of the Allies failed; Hitler was always too well protected, too well guarded.

Most leaders around the world rely on one, maybe two bodyguards to keep them safe. Even the President of the United States today has only one or two teams of security personnel; while there may be many men and women who take turns to protect their leader, the numbers are not as big as you would expect it to be.

In contrast, Hitler had *thousands* of men – he had entire armies built just to keep him safe. No wonder no attempt on his life ever came into fruition!

In this book, we will take a look at the many different organizations that served under Hitler as part of his protection detail.

They all evolved from being just his bodyguards to setting up a dictator-like regime in Nazi-controlled Europe; where they were begun as a body to keep him safe, they soon turned to military operations under his control and began to do his bidding while still protecting him.

We will look at the origins of a number of bodies, such as the 'Sturmabteilung' or the SA, the Schutzstaffel (the SS) and the many other sub-sections of the SS such as the FBK, the LSSAH, etc., all of which were tasked with protecting Hitler.

From the background, we will move on to individual accounts of men who served on these teams – they were Hitler's personal bodyguards and some stayed with him until the very end.

Humanity's depraved nature came to fore with these men; despite having a master who was truly mad and ravenous for blood, they served him loyally. Was it because they were also as depraved as he was? Or were they afraid for their lives and did what they had to, to survive? We can only wonder...

CHAPTER 1

BACKGROUND OF THE WAR AND THE CONCEPTION OF THE BODYGUARD ORGANIZATIONS

When the First World War came to an end in the year 1918, Adolf Hitler was just a young man of 29 years who was frustrated, bitter and angry over his country's defeat at the hands of the Allied Powers. Like a number of the German people, particularly the veterans, he also adhered to the Stab-in-the-Back Myth that was floating around at the time.

To give you a little bit of background, this Stab-in-the-Back Myth was basically a euphemism for the Anti-Semitist Attitudes of the time. A lot of people believed that Germany lost the war due to its communists and the Jews – the right-wing circles of the country propagated the idea that World War I was lost not because of the lack of prowess on the battlefield, but because some civilians had betrayed them from within their own borders.

Of these a majority of them had been Jews, claimed the right-wing activists, thereby adding to the unrest that was already stirring within the country.

The 1930s came around, and with them, the Great Depression begun. Germany suffered from acute economic crises; the hatred against the Jews grew, with many believing that had Germany won the war, they wouldn't be in such a sad state at this point.

In truth, the Germans were simply looking for someone to take the blame, so they could take their frustrations out on them – the Jews provided an excellent outlet for this.

It was into this turbulent political scenario that Hitler stepped – a number of extremist Germans came together to form the German Workers' Party, the DAP, which was the forerunner of the Nazi Party. Hitler joined these men and with his oratorical skills and his charisma, he managed to rise through the ranks far quicker than anyone could have expected out of such a diminutive little man.

And as he grew in power, so did his paranoia about being killed – he surrounded himself with more men that one could possibly expect, with thousands of soldiers acting as his bodyguards.

Given that his speeches, despite being spectacularly delivered and reasoned out, basically incited violence and racist tendencies, it's not surprising that he became so worried for his own life.

Of the many organizations that took charge of Hitler's protection detail, the first was the SA – the Sturmabteilung. They were the first group of men to perform paramilitary techniques in protection of the Fuhrer, though they soon evolved into an elite group that provided protection for a number of Nazi officials, all of whom were in high military command positions.

They were formed in the year 1920 and served as the forerunners of all the other protective details that would follow.

Soon after, in the year 1923, the SSH or the Stosstrupp-Hitler was created. It was set up especially to protect the Fuhrer and was in direct control of the men of the SA. As the Nazi Party grew in numbers, however, it became obvious that a lot more men were needed to make sure that all the generals and the officials remained safe from any and all attempts to assassinate them.

Thus came about the Schutzstaffel or the SS, which is the most well-known police protection force of the Second World War. They were also begun as part of the SA initially – their first duty was the protection of Hitler. When they came into being, they were only about one hundred men or so in number; later, they evolved into a massive body of soldiers to be reckoned with.

As the SS grew, different factions of it served as Hitler's personal command at different times. The Führerbegleitkommando or the FBK, Leibstandarte SS Adolf Hitler or the LSSAH and the Reichssicherheitsdienst or the RDS – these were the primary forces that looked out for the Furher on a regular basis. All three organizations were begun as subsets of the SS.

And while these factions generally served as his personal protection detail, there were also times when Hitler called upon the bigger, more spread out organizations. These police forces generally were tasked with the sniffing out of Jews and all other 'criminals' within the country and questioning and taking them into custody.

The Gestapo, or the Geheime Staatspolizei, is the most well known of these bodies; there were also the Ordnungspolizei or the Orpo, the Kriminalpolizei or the Kripo and the Sicherheitspolizei, also known as the SiPo. They all served under the SS and responded to any calls sent out to keep the Nazis and Hitler safe at any time.

If these men were not enough, there was even an intelligence organization that was formed. They were called Sicherheitsdienst or the SD. They did not always interact with Hitler's protection detail directly, but their job remained the same – sniff out any people who might want to harm the Furher.

In time, however, they began to expand their duties to search for any unwanted elements within German society – Jews, homosexuals, Allied spies, etc. They would personally investigate these people, do background checks on them, conduct random security checks and the like; not even Party members were exempt from this kind of a thorough verification.

Once they were done sniffing into a person's past, they would decide whether he or she were a 'desirable' element of Hitler's Germany. If they were not – or they posed any kind of threat to the Furher – the SD would instantly send a message out to the Gestapo, who would then go over and make the arrest on their behalf.

Needless to say, after a while, it became less about 'security checks' and more about personal racism and vendettas.

But then, the same could be said of Hitler's entire campaign and the whole of the Second World War. The Nazis' racism and their anger towards a few communities they did not understand formed the basis of the war itself; they tortured, maimed and killed millions of innocent people who had done nothing wrong.

It shocked the whole world – with the introduction of what Hitler called 'The Final Solution to the Jewish Problem', the Allied Powers stepped up their own attacks.

They had no choice but to do so; hundreds of thousands of innocent people – men, women and children – were getting gassed to death and sent to concentration camps without a shred of mercy. And if they were not sent to be killed, they were being used as lab rats for men such as Joseph Mengele to perform strange and disturbing experiments on.

The Allies, aware of all this, did everything they could to bring Hitler down – the number of assassination attempts on the Furher went up, desperate as they were to cut off the head of the snake before it could strike them down.

But they were to remain completely unsuccessful. Hitler knew his life was in danger; he was a smart and intelligent man who had managed to amass so much power within so short a time with only the help of his own oratorical skill. He knew how to take advantage of the situation around him – despite being no one special, he rose in ranks to become the most powerful man in Germany.

Whatever he was, he was not stupid, which was how he knew that he had to form so many bodyguard organizations to make sure the Allies could not get to him.

And they didn't – the ring of bodyguard leaders in Hitler's inner most circles established a routine that was perfectly suited to keeping the Furher safe. Every place that he went, he took some men from the FBK with him. These men were on shifts; each man worked three eight-hour shifts, at the end of which he would be replaced by one of his comrades.

All of them were extremely well trained and knowledgeable in the art of taking someone down quickly – as Hitler's personal protection; their own lives were in danger if the Furher was even close to any kind of harm.

Before Hitler was to leave on any trip, like going on to attend some public event or something, the RSD would first traverse that route themselves. Their purpose was to make the road as safe for Hitler as it was possible – they would look for weak spots in the route, identify vulnerabilities, check all the buildings, and fix up alternatives in case they needed to make a quick escape.

They would arrive at the destination and check that building from the top to bottom to make sure that the Furher would remain safe through the entirety of his visit.

They wouldn't stop there; the RSD would also make a visit to the local police. The Gestapo in the area were required to provide intelligence of what was happening there; reports were made as to who was doing what and if there was any chatter about assassinations or any kind of threats made to Hitler's life. If there were, the RSD would often call the Orpo officers to help them beef up security.

All the streets were lined with men from the SS – they were required to wear uniforms to show that they were part of Hitler's entourage. Every entry, every exit and every single way into a building was guarded by these men; Hitler did not just make use of them for his own protection, but also wanted to send a message to anyone who would dare to oppose him – here, take a look, I've got an entire army of men to keep me safe, don't try anything!

Every third man of this group faced the crowd; the marksmen and the sharp shooters were stationed on the roof. In the meantime, the RSD officers, dressed in plain clothes would blend in with the crowd below that was waiting for their Furher to make an appearance.

This way, they could scope for threats discreetly and they were often joined by the undercover police force from the Kripo.

All this was simply prep for Hitler's arrival, which, by itself, was quite a fanfare. In front of his motorcade, a single pilot car would drive in first, which the guards would take as a cue to get into position and stand at attention for their ruler.

Hitler himself would usually arrive in a Mercedes-Benz with an open hood – he preferred to be seated or standing in the front seat and visible to all so that the Germans and the Nazis could take note of the man leading them. His car would be 50 meters behind the pilot car, explicitly plotted out, with his security kept at the forefront.

Obviously, it wasn't the most defendable or safe position, next to the driver seat, but the SS managed. An FBK member would always be behind him, and behind his car, two more would follow, one flanking his left side and the other flanking his right.

These cars also had detachments of RSD soldiers who were ready to jump into action at a moment's notice. Behind these cars, Nazi commanders and any other SS leaders who had accompanied them followed, and another 100 meters behind those cars arrived any foreign guests they were hosting.

This was only in the case of Hitler's travel alone; his offices and his residences were an entirely different matter. The LSSAH handled those sections of his security – they acted as the outer ring of safety and defense for the Furher, particularly when he was hosting visitors.

They protected buildings such as the old and the new Reich Chancellery, the Berghof in the Bavarian Alps of Bavaria, etc. The LSSAH soldiers took their places at the entrances and the exits to the Old and New Reich Chancellery, where they acted as sentries.

They were augmented by the Orpo police, who took up sentry posts inside the building – they checked the crowd's entry passes as well as their identity cards to make sure that there were no spies or enemies entering the building.

The Gestapo and Kripo also provided security; they reported directly to the RSD, especially when it came to running any background and security checks on the employees or workers. The SD also kept an eye on things; they were on constant look out for subversive and spy activities and any suspicious information gathered, they sent to the Gestapo who were then able to take action and arrest the suspicious individuals.

If Hitler was in the building, then both the RSD and FBK were around. The former set of men went on regular patrols of the ground, whereas the latter men were in charge of providing personal and close security protection to the Furher.

In case a special event was being hosted, the number of LSSAH guards who were on duty went up. To make sure that they would be available for work at a moment's notice, barracks for them to sleep and live in were set up at the Berghof residence; this meant that a large number of soldiers were ready to protect Hitler whenever he called on them without any hesitation whatsoever.

Not only did they jump on scene when the Furher asked, they spent all their time going on rounds and patrols to ensure safety for a large security zone around the building – this section, cordoned off from the public view, was the place where a number of higher Nazi officials lived.

As I mentioned previously, Hitler's bodyguards soon went from protecting him alone to defending high-up Nazi commanders too; this security zone was one of those places where they lived and made use of Hitler's guards for their own personal defense.

To add to that, the RSD was also housed in the same area; a hotel that was nearby was quickly turned into a base for them, so they lived and operated out of it, ready to fly to the defense of both Nazi leaders and Hitler at any second of any day.

With all that protection detail, it is easy to understand how Hitler never managed to get hurt from all the assassination attempts. Let me give you one simple example to demonstrate how well his security personnel performed.

This is the infamous Reichssicherheitsdienst incident – it was how the RSD came to be given command of Hitler's personal security detail. In the year 1933, one night, Hitler was in the city of Munich. It was not long before the Furher, ever sharp and observant, identified that there was a car that was following their own.

He told his driver – Eric Kempka – to press down on the accelerator pedal. The Mercedes-Benz had been supercharged and was equipped to go at extremely fast speeds to enable more safety and defense for Hitler, and he believed that it would not be able to keep up.

But then, the car did not vanish; it managed to keep up with him. Later on, it came to the Furher's notice that the car was not an enemy, but his own men! The RSD, who were his personal bodyguards, had taken it upon themselves to provide protection for him even without his own knowledge.

They simply had not told him or any of the men traveling with him that they were taking such a big step.

When it came to his knowledge that the RSD had done such a thing, Hitler was initially very furious. The Bavarian police was not a force he was fond of; he trusted them very little since there had been an attempt on his life under their watch and it had almost succeeded. With this act, he was done – he wanted to get rid of the RSD completely.

It was his second in command, a man named Himmler, who was put in charge of a huge number of men and usually took control of Hitler's personal guard, who talked him out of it.

He told Hitler that he would establish changes in the way the RSD was run, that he would improve their orders and the way they operated. Truth be told, he was quite impressed at the way they followed Hitler and offered him protection – once the Furher was calmed down and agreed to keep them on, Himmler reorganized the RSD.

Then onwards, the RSD took control of Hitler's personal security and managed to keep him safe from all kinds of threats. The Allies tried time and again to assassinate this depraved Head of the Nazis, but he was untouchable – he was always surrounded by hundreds of men who were trained to give up their lives for him at a moment's notice.

No matter how hard the Allied Powers tried, they could not get to him; the SS and all the other factions who handled his security detail always thwarted them.

With such a large force under his command for his protection, that comes as no surprise!

CHAPTER 2

BODYGUARD ORGANIZATIONS

As I have told you before, Hitler had not one or two men, not even just a dozen bodyguards, but entire organizations that handled his protective detail. He would never take a chance with his own life; he knew he had enemies and took every precaution to keep himself safe and sound.

To that extent, he built an empire of soldiers – let us take a look at the different organizations that evolved from being his bodyguards to paramilitary troops that augmented the Nazis.

The Sturmabteilung – Storm Detachment (SA)

As we saw in the previous chapter, this was one of the very first bodyguard organizations that Hitler set up. It came into being in the year 1920 and was a paramilitary organization as a group to protect all the Nazis. Their sole purpose in the beginning was to police party rallies – they had to go and disrupt any meetings the opposing parties were conducting.

When the Nazis took power and control of the State in the year 1933, the SA had grown massively – where once there were only a few hundred, now they had grown to a shocking number of almost four million men.

Hitler placed Ernst Röhm, one of the men who had backed him during his earlier days in the newly-formed Nazi Party, at the helm of the SA and together, they took Germany by storm.

But all was not well for the contingent of soldiers or Röhm. Soon after Hitler came into power and was named Chancellor of Germany, Hitler grew paranoid at the strength and the independence that the SA had consolidated for itself.

At the time, it was the single most efficient and powerful group of soldiers around, other than the Nazis themselves. Their influence on the German population was enormous. And unfortunately for him, some of the leaders did not appreciate Hitler's actions – they were outspoken about the redistribution of wealth and a second revolution that would follow the Nazis' own rise to power.

This led to what is known today as the Night of the Long Knives; Hitler moved against many members of the SA, including Röhm, and had them all 'purged'.

The killings were carried out by the SS and the Gestapo and the purge strengthened his position twice fold – he no longer had any opposition within the country and he proved his mantle as autocratic dictator by taking out those who would dare to speak out against him.

The Stosstrupp-Hitler – Shock Troop-Hitler (SSH)

A small and separate bodyguard unit, the SSH was formed in the year

1923. It came into being on Hitler's singular orders and unlike the SA, which had to serve the entire Nazi Party, the SSH's only aim was to look out for Hitler himself.

It was dedicated to the service of the Furher and was not a 'suspect mass' of the party. When it was started, it had only eight men in the team – they were headed by Julius Schreck and Joseph Berchtold.

Named the Stabswache or the staff guard, they were given badges that were unique to them. However, even when they received their badges and were told to protect Hitler, they were still under the overall control of the SA.

It was Schreck who decided to use the Totenkopf, or the death's head sign, as the unit's personal insignia – it was a symbol that most people associated with power and strength, given that the most elite forces in the Prussian, and later the German Empire, till then had made use of.

It was not until the month of May in the year 1923 that the unit came to be known as Stosstrupp-Hitler – with Schreck in command, the unit served as Hitler's personal protection and every man in it was considered to be a Hitler loyalist. The unit never had more than 20 men at one time and their members included notable names like Sepp Dietrich and Walter Buch.

In a way, the disbanding of the SSH was what allowed Hitler to complete the consolidation of his power within Germany and take his place at its helm. On the 9th of November, 1923, the SSH, with the help of the SA and a number of other Nazi units, were part of the abortive Beer Hall Putsch that took place in Munich. Also known as the Munich Putsch, it was a coup attempt that failed.

Hitler moved to seize control of Munich, Bavaria – more than two thousand men marched into the center of the city and confronted the police. A number of Nazis and policemen were killed in the scuffle and

Hitler himself did not escape injury during the battle.

This was when he was arrested and taken into custody – the SSH was disbanded and Hitler was imprisoned for nine months afterwards.

But this was a move that brought him attention; with his arrest, the putsch brought to notice of the German people as well as the outside world, that he was a man willing to do whatever was necessary to assume control. The 24 day trial that came after his arrest was widely publicized – smart as a whip, Hitler used this as a platform to spread his agenda.

He managed to bring to the people his nationalist sentiments and his oratorical skills were good enough that he convinced millions of people of his ideology.

Word began to spread like wildfire about his strength and his politics; he himself was found guilty and sent to prison with a sentence of five years. While in jail, he worked on his Mein Kampf, his infamous ideology – outside, the people began to accept him as their ruler and began to spread his political thought and gather support for him.

With his arrest, he cemented his rise to power; instead of the five years he was sent in for, he was released in just nine months, after which he became undisputed leader of Germany.

Schutzstaffel – Protection Squadron (SS)

Today, it is the SS that is synonymous with the Nazi party, but it is the SS that was begun as the protective detail that would protect Hitler. When the SA was begun, it grew into an organization that numbered millions of soldiers, the SS started with less than just a hundred men.

The uniform of the SS became infamous – anyone wearing a black tie and a black cap that had the Totenkopf or the 'death's head', which was basically skull and bones, symbol on it were understood to be as part of the SS.

Unlike the SA, which was relatively easier to get into, the SS had a number of stricter rules and restrictions and candidates would have to go through a long drawn out process to be able to join them. Given that their purpose was the protection of Hitler himself, this is not very surprising.

What is interesting to note is that the SS remained subordinate to the SA for a while, up until the summer of the year 1934. However, despite that, they considered themselves better than the SA – since getting in was most difficult and their true purpose was different from the others, they behaved as though they were an elite class of soldiers, not really a part of the SS as such.

In January 1929, Heinrich Himmler took control of the SS when he took command as Reichsführer-SS before he went on to become the chief of all the German police forces.

The SS grew in number slowly and a number of factions developed even within itself. The main, well known branches of the SS were the Allgemeine SS, SS-Totenkopfverbände and the Waffen-SS. Of these, the Waffen-SS is perhaps the most well-known; they were the ones most often on the scene and most active around the country.

Apart from these three main branches, there were also a number of sub-branches, including but not limited to the RSHA or the Reich Main Security Office, which had a number of departments of its own for the other police forces, such as the Gestapo and the Kripo.

Later, once the war ended, a number of surveys were conducted. Data collected, along with the details released about the judgments that were delivered at the Nuremberg War Trials, it was found that the SS was behind most of the crimes the Nazis committed.

Not for nothing are they the most well-known of all Nazi commands – they were the primary front for the Holocaust as a whole.

Sicherheitsdienst – Security Service (SD)

SD was that organization of security personnel that handled the intelligence side of things. Initially, they were subordinate only to the SS and reported any chatter against Hitler personally to the SS higher ups.

But as time passed and they grew in number, the need for reliable intelligence also grew – they began to cater to the Nazi Party as a whole and performed intelligence services for all of Germany.

It was Himmler, again, who founded the SD – he began it in the year 1931 as the Ic-Dienst and handed control of the organization to Reinhard Heydrich. In the year 1934, by the month of April, it began to be considered as the sister organization of the Gestapo and was renamed Sicherheitsdienst.

Where the SD did the gathering of the information and intelligence, the Gestapo – along with the help of the Kripo – went around acting on the intelligence so collected. Thus, the SD remained the information gathering agency, while the Gestapo took over the execution of the political systems that did the police work.

Even though they were, technically, under the control of Heydrich, the SD – and incidentally, the Gestapo too – answered to Himmler as a whole, given that he was appointed as the Chief of German Police. By the time the year 1944 rolled around, the SD had managed to multiply into an organization that contained more than 6000 members – when Heydrich died, it was Ernst Kaltenbrunner who took over command of the SD.

Führerschutzkommando (FSK), Reichssicherheitsdienst (RSD) and Führerbegleitkommando (FBK)

These three organizations are the ones that handled a majority of Hitler's personal protection. They were the men he trusted the most, to the point that as long as they were with him, they did not need to surrender their weapons and wouldn't be asked to provide any kind of identification.

Obviously, this meant that getting to be part of these elite squads was a long drawn out process that not every person could achieve.

The evolution of these three organizations is quite fascinating; before the FBK came into being, it was only the FSK. Both find their roots in their parent organization, the SS-Begleitkommando des Führers or the Escort Commander of the Furher. Shortened as SS-Begleitkommando, this was an elite team, consisting of eight men, who were picked out of the SS for what Hitler called 'their outstanding loyalty'.

They were begun in the month of February, 1932 and their initial purpose was to be Hitler's protection escort as he travelled from one place to another.

These men served around the clock in three eight-hour shifts. What is interesting is that their duties were expansive and included not only Hitler's own protection but also general safety and defense for other functionaries of the Nazi Party. At the very beginning, twelve men were handpicked and then presented to Hitler – he chose the eight of them who would accompany him on his travels and then gave them the name SS-Begleitkommando des Führers.

A little while later, when the spring of the year 1934 came around, the SS-Begleitkommando des Führers stopped taking responsibility for Hitler's overall protection and narrowed their work down to only personal protection wherever he went.

Instead of them, the Führerschutzkommando or the FSK took over and handled his overall defense. They would do the planning of routes, building checks, etc., while the smaller unit of eight men would serve as Hitler's immediate protection wherever he went.

The FSK were the ones who were responsible for the overall, general security measures – many a time, it was their preventive measures which saved Hitler's life from assassination attempts. They were also the men in charge of prosecuting these assassins.

It was the FSK that was turned into the Reichssicherheitsdienst or the Reich Security Service (RSD). This happened on the 1st of August in the year 1935 and they remained the RSD until the end of the war.

Meanwhile the small unit SS-Begleitkommando was still in charge of Hitler's personal protection; they worked in tandem with the newly formed RSD, along with the Orpo, the Gestapo and other agencies to handle the inner security for Hitler. In the meantime, the outer and general security was provided by the general SS units.

It was not long before the SS-Begleitkommando began to expand and turned into the Führerbegleitkommando or the FBK. These men were personally under Hitler's command and provided his close security for him alone. The additional members that were added to the initially eight-man unit were drawn from the LSSAH, which we shall take a look at in the next section.

Hitler not only made use of them as his own personal bodyguards but also as valets, waiters, couriers and even orderlies. They were his to use and to command, and although they were technically and administratively under the command of the LSSAH, their orders came from Hitler directly, and later on, from Julius Schaub, his chief adjutant.

As I said previously, these men were so trusted by Hitler that he kept them around him at all times. When they were on duty, the FBK were the only armed soldiers he would let near him – they never gave up their pistols and as long as they were with him, they were never searched or given the same treatment as any of the other SS soldiers.

Although the FBK worked with the RSD to protect and keep Hitler safe during all the public trips and events, the FBK never considered themselves to be part as the RSD – in fact, they operated as two separate groups, even going so far as to maintain two different vehicles for transport during the events themselves.

The head of the RSD, Johann Rattenhuber, was the overall commander, and it was the FBK Chief who worked as his deputy. To further make them part of the SS collective, they were soon made to wear the same standard field grey uniform of the SS – they were technically under the command of the SS only and their members did have SS origins.

The last of the FBK commanders was Franz Schadle, who served in his capacity as SS-Obersturmbannführer in the year 1945. He took his post after Burno Gesche was dismissed. Schadle and his men went with Hitler and his entourage wherever he went.

Leibstandarte SS Adolf Hitler (LSSAH)

The Life Guards SS Adolf Hitler was the other major organization that handled his protection and defense. It was founded in the year 1933 as a palace guard at the beginning – these men were meant to offer protection for all of Hitler's offices and his residences.

It goes without saying that the LSSAH, as Hitler's personal guards, required the most difficult of training regimens and steps to join. Not only did they want men to be in tip top physical health and condition, they were also expected to be young, in between the ages of 25 to 35 so that they had agility and mobility.

Add to this the fact that they had to produce a confirmed ancestry record – Hitler wanted no person of Jewish origin to even come close to him. Even a great grandfather somewhere on the tree, hundreds of years ago, would get them rejected.

As the LSSAH grew, it became bigger and bigger and eventually turned into a more elite class of the SS itself. Unlike the FBK or the RSD, these men answered to Hitler, but their direct orders came from Sepp Dietrich, who was the real commander and took care of the administrative activities of the day to day.

When the War began in earnest and the front lines required men to lead, it was the LSSAH that were sent there in the year 1945 – it had grown that big and could easily be an army of its own. Of all the men who were picked to be part of the LSSAH, a core group of 800 or so men were elected to stay back while the rest of them went to wage war; these men were made to stay in Berlin and formed the Leibstandarte Guard Battalion, which was assigned to protect the Furher alone.

Geheime Staatspolizei (Gestapo)

Other than the SS themselves, it is the Gestapo that is known as the most active force of the Nazi Party during the Second World War. Called the Secret State Police, they were everything they were named to be – the Nazis used them as the secret police force in all areas they occupied.

They came into being in the month of April in 1933 and were formed by the aviation minister who went by the name of Hermann Goring. The next year saw it fall under the administration of the SS and it soon came to be seen as the sister organization of the SD.

Their purpose was simple – draw on members of all agencies and then build a huge network of spies and informants who would be able to speak for what was happening in Nazi occupied Germany and other parts of Europe. They were headed by Heydrich and Heinrich Muller.

Now, what is interesting about the Gestapo is how utterly cruel and merciless the Gestapo were.

Yes, it is a given that they would internalize the values and behavior systems that they saw around them and what they saw around them was a belief that the Jews and other communities were lower than them and had to be discriminated against.

However, the cruelty they displayed in treating them went beyond that – they were not bothered if people died during their 'interrogations' and they tortured them mercilessly when it came to gathering information.

What made it worse was that they had been given a type of power known as the Schutzhaft or the 'protective custody'. This basically meant that they could take anyone in on any suspicion – it was a euphemistic way of saying that there need not be any judicial or court proceedings when it came to arresting people they were suspicious of.

It goes without saying that too many innocents were thus thrown in jail without even verifying the validity of the Gestapo's claims. This way, up until the end of the Second War, the Gestapo managed to be the driving force behind the entire Nazi Party.

Ordnungspolizei (Orpo)

The Order Police or the Orpo was the forefront of the Gestapo; where the latter force was a secret network of spies operating from underground, the Orpo were those police officers in uniforms who patrolled the streets of Nazi Germany.

They were formulated in the year 1936 by the interior ministry – they were the proper policemen who were tasked with the responsibility of maintaining law and order through the country.

Initially under the command of a police general named Kurt Daluege, the power then moved hands when he was struck down by a heart attack – Alfred Wunnenburg replaced him in the year 1943. Within the next year, the organization grew exponentially; it ended up having more than 400,000 members, thereby taking its place as the organization with the biggest police force in the German nation.

Like the Gestapo, the Orpo were also often called upon by the more elite protective forces like the FSK and the FBK to provide support whenever and wherever Hitler was traveling; they provided the manpower as the government required.

Kriminalpolizei (Kripo)

A corollary of the Orpo, the Kripo were the criminal police task force of the Nazi Party. These men were more or less the detectives of the force; they wore plain clothes and blended in with the crowd to search for threats from the insides. They worked in tandem with the Gestapo and conducted searches and gathered intelligence under the guise of normal people.

Like the Orpo and the Gestapo, the Kripo also usually provided support when Hitler was traveling. If, for instance, there was a public speaking event where the Furher was making an appearance, the entire security process would be handled by the RSD – the FBK would keep around the Furher and protect him personally. The Orpo and Gestapo would give the extra security while the Kripo would be hiding out within the crowd and scoping out threats from the other side.

Sicherheitspolizei (SiPo)

The Security Police or the SiPo was the criminal investigative division of the Nazi Party. It came into being in the year 1936 and drew its men from both the Kripo and the Gestapo, combining their skillset and their abilities to form perfect criminal detectives.

Again, like the Orpo, Kripo and Gestapo, the SiPo also provided support to the elite divisions when they required it – however, unlike its sister organizations, it did not last very long.

Within three years of its formulation, in the year 1939, it was amassed into the Reichssicherheitshauptamt or the Reich Main Security Office (RSHA) and became part of that organization instead.

Führer Begleitbattalion (FBB)

The Furher Escort Battalion or the FBB was a military unit that was set up for the Furher's protection just before the Second World War began in earnest. It was begun with the purpose of keeping Hitler's military headquarters safe – they also went with him when he visited the battlefronts.

As the name suggests, their duty was limited to the military side of things; Hitler's residence and the like were defended by the FBK and the RSD, while the FBB took care of him when he was in the vicinity of anything militia.

When it started, it had only a hundred men or so and was headed by the infantry colonel Erwin Rommel. Later on, as it grew, Otto Ernst Remer took charge of it, taking the expanded FBB and training them well. They became so strong that they were one of the key players who took down all those involved in the military coup of 20 July 1944 in Berlin, which attempted to overthrow Hitler once and for all.

These were the many organizations that handled Hitler's protection detail during the course of the Second World War. As you can see, no other leader in history has ever had such an expansive and extensive network of soldiers dedicated to his defense – by the time the war came to an end, there were hundreds of thousands of men who were willing to die to keep him safe.

No wonder then, that the Allies could not touch him; he was protected by the strongest, meanest and most powerful men Nazi Germany could offer.

In the next few chapters, let us take a look at some of the individual soldiers who were part of these organizations. We will look at their stories, their contribution to Hitler's protection and what roles they played in the War itself.

CHAPTER 3

KURT GILDISCH – LOST TO THE BOTTLE

Hitler's men were some of the strongest, meanest and the most powerful men in the world, but that did not exempt them from their own vices. In fact, in many ways, they were their own enemies – not only did their lives reflect the cruel nature of their racist, supremist ideologies, they also ended up shooting themselves in the foot trying to please a man who would condemn a person for simply being who they were.

Kurt Gildisch was a soldier, handpicked to be part of Hitler's personal guard, who ended up ruining his own life and career due to his drinking problem.

He was, in fact, the third commander of Hitler's bodyguards, the SS-Begleitkommando des Führers, and came from a teaching background; unable to find a job as a teacher, he took to the police force. He initially worked as part of the Prussian Police, who gave him the boot after his Nazi connections came into light.

Following this, he joined the SA and became a Nazi in full. What is interesting is his career as part of the Nazi Party; he served in the SA, joined the SS, became the head commander of the SS-Begleitkommando and then was kicked out to fight at the frontlines, following which he was released and then went out to lead a life of drunkenness until his re-arrest later and his death.

Let us take a look at it all in detail.

Kurt Gildisch was born in March of the year 1902, in a small village called Potrempschen, which is located in the Eastern Part of Prussia, about 23 kilometers south west of Insterburg. He came by his profession of teaching genetically – his father was a schoolteacher, who insisted that he attend primary school in the village and get his degree in teaching.

As a result, he studied whatever his own village offered him and then moved to the nearby, bigger town of Insterburg, where he trained to be a teacher till the year 1922. In the year 1924, he took the test meant for certifying school teachers.

However, it so happened that there were few vacancies in the field when he started looking for jobs. He could not find himself a good school to teach in and tired from the lack of opportunities, he went ahead and applied for a job with the Prussian police force.

In the year 1925, he was then sent to the police school which was located in Sensburg. He studied there from January to September and graduated with the qualification to get an accelerated promotion to the position of officer. A month later, in October 1925, he was then moved to the city of Berlin.

But this was where all his problems seem to have begun. Despite having graduated with a good stand and having even received an accelerated advancement to officer, Gildisch had a drinking problem. He drank too much and had a number of episodes with his superiors and given that he often came into work hung over, he was eyed extremely suspiciously by the rest of his officers.

The suspicions came to a head when his ties to the Nazi Party came out into the fore. The Prussian police force found out that his sympathies lay with the Nazis and he was looking at their ideologies and propagating their agenda; they gave him the boot.

In the month of March of the year 1931, Gildisch was kicked out of the police force, with his Nazi affiliations being cited as the official reason. It is possible that his drinking problem also had something to do with it, though this was never truly confirmed.

But Gildisch found this to be an opportunity instead of a tragedy; given that he had been kicked for being associated with the Nazi Party, he decided to make it an official thing. A month after the Prussian police kicked him out, on the 1st of April; he went and signed up for the SA, where he remained for a few months before he was moved to the SS on the 29th of September that same year.

Gildisch served in the SS for some time, quickly rising through the ranks, until the month of February in 1932 rolled around. Heinrich Himmler, who was now slowly consolidating power as one of Hitler's second in commands, advised him to personally pick out eight out of twelve men to serve as his bodyguards.

These 12 men had been selected by Sepp Dietrich and all of them were part of the SS. They had been tested for physical, mental and emotional strength – they were said to be the most loyal of all the SS soldiers.

Gildisch was one of these 12 men. And soon enough, when he was presented to Hitler as part of the team, he was personally chosen as one of the SS-Begleitkommando des Führers. Now the problem was that even though it had been his idea from the very beginning, Himmler did not like the eight men who were under Hitler's control.

This could be because they did not take their orders from him; technically, he was in charge of them, but Gildisch and these other men reported directly to the Furher and took their direct orders from him only. It could be possible that he saw this as a usurping of his power or that he expected to be given complete control of them, which he was not.

Given that Himmler did not like any of the men and that he was eyeing them like a hawk, Gildisch was definitely on thin ice already. His drinking problem was getting worse and worse as the days went by; despite that, he was made head of the small unit and spent all his days protecting the Furher, taking orders from Hitler himself and reporting to him directly.

Although Gildisch was technically outranked by Himmler, since he took his command from Hitler directly, Himmler was not fond of him at all. Gildisch's entire command was above Himmler in this manner – it annoyed the general to no end and he kept an eye out for some reason to bring the man down, which came soon enough.

Gildisch's drinking, growing steadily bad, soon got the best of him and he was coming to work drunk or hung over more often than not.

On the 15th of June in the year 1934, Himmler went above Gildisch and had him removed – he cited that Gildisch was a heavy drinker and could not be trusted. A drunkard was no leader and had no strength to lead what was supposed to be the most powerful and most difficult of protection teams; they were to guard the Furher himself, so how could they trust the safety of Nazi Germany's leader to a man like him?

It did not take long for him to convince the other commanders – Gildisch was removed and Bruno Gesche took his place as the head of SS-Begleitkommando des Führers. And despite the loyal service Gildisch had provided, Hitler did not interfere and let Himmler have his way.

Gildisch's problems did not end there. Obviously, the expulsion made his drinking problem that much worse – he was skating on thin ice, having been demoted from the unit to just the level of a normal soldier and was repeatedly warned to stop his drinking. However, he refused to do so; he continued to drown his sorrows in the bottle, coming to work each day with a hangover at the very least.

Still, despite the fact that he was no longer part of Hitler's own bodyguard entourage, he still had people who seemed to believe in his battle prowess. From the 30th of June to the 2nd of July in 1934 lasted the Night of the Long Knives.

For those unaware, this was the move that cinched Hitler's power as absolute leader of Germany – he took any and all people within his own party and otherwise whom he felt were against him. That included a number of his own supporters, who had been by his side as he rose to power through the Nazi Ranks.

Now Gildisch was a key player in the Night of the Long Knives – Reinhard Heydrich gave him the order to go to Dr. Erich Klausener's office, where he was to shoot the man and kill him.

Klausener was part of the Prussian Ministry and he was the leader of the Anti-Nazi Katholische Aktion or the Anti-Nazi Catholic Action group that opposed Nazi ideals. Gildisch performed the mission successfully; he took out the doctor as ordered and returned home victorious, unaware that this mission would be the cause of strife for his life much, much later at the war's end.

Once the killing was over, he was promoted to the rank of SS-Sturmbannführer, but that still did not bring his drinking down to an end. If anything, it went worse.

Obviously, it goes without saying that his superiors were not pleased – they soon had him thrown out of the Nazi Party as well as the SS, leading to an even worse bout of drinking and depression.

But the War was running in earnest and the Allied Powers were making their move – the battlefront needed more soldiers to hold up Germany's defense. As the April of the year 1941 rolled around, Gildisch took part in a leadership course – the course was conducted at an SS Junker School that was located in Bad Tolz.

It brought him back into the Nazi fold and he was appointed as the Untersturmführer der Waffen-SS. It was a paramilitary rank and soon, Gildisch was sent to the Eastern Front, where he had to take on the Allied Forces.

From the year 1942, Gildisch fought the war at the battle front and apparently redeemed himself by 'distinguishing himself' in combat, so much so that he was attached to the 11th SS Volunteer Panzergrenadier Division Nordland, which was fighting on the Soviet front of things in the year 1944.

The very same August, he was wounded in battle – a year later, in May 1945, he was again wounded and this time, he was taken into custody by the Soviet army during the Battle of Berlin. He was kept captive therein until the war came to an end.

When the war ended in August of the year 1946, Gildisch was released from prison. Unfortunately, his time inside had not been kind – he had to have his leg amputated since the injury he suffered in battle had only gotten worse. Without a leg, he had no choice but to go in for a prosthetic and ended up limping his way through afterwards.

Even after he was brought back to civilian life, Gildisch could not find a comfortable life. His far-right wing policies meant that he could not find good work; the focus, even within Germany, was slowly shifting to a left-wing perspective of life, with the Allied Powers exerting their influence over the areas they had won and defended.

Gildisch, despite having been thrown out and abandoned by the Nazis, refused to give up on his racist tendencies – his past affiliations to them meant that most people refused to offer him employment, leaving him struggling. However, he retrained as a bookbinder with an Evangelical-Lutheran company who were geared towards employing disabled people and following this training, he managed to find himself a job to get by.

But his life was not meant to be comfortable or happy. In the year 1949, Gildisch was at the Berlin train station, when an old friend recognized him. He had been laying low and hiding his true identity, given that the Allies were slowly rounding up all the men and women who had committed crimes during the War; now his identity was revealed and the police came to arrest him.

He was tried in the Berlin court, where he was put on the stand for the murder of Dr. Erich Klausener.

He was convicted in May of the year 1953 and then sentenced to the next 15 years in prison. His stay there was equally miserable. His heavy drinking meant that his liver was irreparably damaged; he soon fell seriously sick and was transferred to a private hospital. His criminal sentence was suspended because of his poor health and the fact that the jail authorities could not care for him.

Kurt Gildisch thus died in the year 1956 in the private hospital where he was being treated for liver disease. His entire life was a film of tragedy and vice – his right-wing policies left him struggling and although he had a stellar career as bodyguard to Furher himself, he threw it all away for a love of the bottle.

CHAPTER 4

BRUNO GESCHE – THE NINE-RANK FALL

Bruno Gesche, born on the 5th of November in the year 1905, was a lieutenant colonel of the SS and is also one of the most infamous people of Hitler's personal bodyguards. He served as the commander of the FBK, taking over the post after his predecessor – Kurt Gildisch – who was thrown out due to heavy drinking.

What is interesting about Gesche is that he was a right-wing military enthusiast even as early as the First World War. He wanted to make a career in Germany as a military officer; but at the end of World War I, the Treaty of Versailles imposed a number of restrictions on Germany that limited a number of the post-War defenses of Germany.

Added to this was the fact that his own education was limited – he had little prospects when the War drew to a close and began to struggle to make a living.

Fortunately for him, it was around that time that the Anti-Semitism prevalent in society was picking up; at the fringe, the DAP, which was the forerunner of the Nazi Party, was beginning a political movement that was garnering support from all the discontent German citizens who were mistaken blaming the Jews for the defeat of Germany at the hands of the Allies during the First World War. Gesche went ahead and joined the Sturmabteilung or the SA in the year 1922.

When he joined the SA, he was working for a bank – he continued this job for a while until it came to public knowledge that he supported the Nazis. Once the bank found out that he was a member of the SA and had been appointed as Alte Kampfer (which is the term used to denote the older members of the Nazi Party, literally translated into Old Fighter and a reference to all those who joined the party as it was just being conceptualized; in short, its earliest members), they showed him the door and kicked him out of his job.

For Gesche, however, like Kurt Gildisch, this being fired from his job turned out to be a real opportunity in disguise.

For the next two and a half decades, he would serve the Nazis in various capacities, going right up to being the head of command for all the men who protected Hitler personally. As soon as he lost his job, he turned his attention fully to the SA, devoting all his time and energy into completing whatever they wanted him to do.

It was not until the year 1927 that he chose to leave the SA for the SS, which, at that time, was still in its early organizational setup of the SSH, functioning as Hitler's future bodyguard. It soon turned into the SS-Begleitkommando des Führers, of which he would form an integral part.

As we saw in the previous chapter of Gildisch, it was the Reichsführer-SS, Heinrich Himmler, who advised Hitler to pick out a team of men to serve as his own personal bodyguard team. Sepp Dietrich presented a team of twelve men to the Furher, who chose eight of them himself and of these eight, Gesche was one.

Gildisch also served at the same time as him, and just like his predecessor, Himmler also disliked Gesche. And this tiff between them would end up defining Gesche's fate through the rest of the Third Reich.

The problem was that, unlike his predecessor, Gesche was a man who had a somewhat personal relationship with Hitler. The Furher was fond of the soldier; both Hitler and Gesche knew one another from their olden days at the NSDAP when the Nazi Party was just turning out – Hitler remembered him from their days as old guard comrades.

Unfortunately for Gesche, this meant that he received Hitler's personal attention more often than not, a fact that irritated Himmler to no end. Himmler did not like either Gesche or Gildisch and did everything he could to get both of them demoted and thrown out of the FBK.

Another reason Himmler probably was not fond of Gesche was the fact that even though the SS-Begleitkommando des Führers were supposed to be under his control, the men took their orders directly from Hitler himself.

Given that he was the one who came up with the idea of a personal guard in the first place, it is possible that he expected to be given command of them – on paper, they were, but in reality, they were to report to Hitler directly.

The first major reported incident between Himmler and Gesche took place in October of the year 1932. Hitler was to deliver a campaign speech in the town of Selb in Bavaria and it goes without saying that the SS-Begleitkommando des Führers, with Gesche at the forefront, were in charge of Hitler's security during this time.

Himmler, who commanded SS and other factions, was in charge of setting up general security and making sure the area was safe for Hitler – Gesche accused that the security detail he provided was not safe enough and criticized him publicly.

Despite the fact that he had Hitler's favor, Gesche seemed to have forgotten that he was still, technically, outranked by Himmler, who took this as an opportunity to have him removed. The accusation stung the fierce general – he took it as a personal insult and did everything he could to have Gesche demoted and taken away from his position at the SS-Begleitkommando des Führers.

But despite that, Hitler ordered that Gesche only be reprimanded – Himmler had no choice but to let him off with a simple warning, which grated on him even more.

Himmler, fortunately for him, did manage to get rid of Gildisch – as we saw earlier, he had him thrown on the excuse of being an alcoholic, thereby not being good enough to be a part of Hitler's personal guard. Gildisch went on to be thrown out of the Nazi Party itself – it was Gesche who replaced him in the SS-Begleitkommando des Führers, taking his post as commander of the small unit, which had begun to grow.

He took the lead in the month of June in the year 1934, and soon after, it was expanded and took on the title of the FBK.

In the following months and years, Gesche's conflict with Himmler would continue as the two would try to one up one another on all fronts. For instance, in the year 1935, Himmler, who was trying very hard to consolidate more and more power – which he felt was owed to him as one of the oldest party members – tried to get Gesche and his men in trouble.

He stated that the personal salaries of all the men serving as Hitler's bodyguard should be suspended, especially since they were already being given food, lodging and comfortable lifestyles as part of their daily routines.

Gesche was not one to be outdone. He retaliated immediately by going to the head of LSSAH, Sepp Dietrich – the LSSAH was the troupe that served as Hitler's personal bodyguard apart from the FBK themselves, and the two organizations worked close together to make sure the Furher remained safe where ever he went. Dietrich, in favor of the men, managed to get the order reversed, thereby ensuring that the men would continue to get paid for doing their jobs.

But like his predecessor, Kurt Gildisch, Bruno Gesche also had a problem – he would often get intoxicated and drink excessively, getting hung over and tired. Himmler once again capitalized on this front; he established an order that was applicable to all the SS men from then on.

In the year 1937, this order came into effect – it stated that all the SS men would not be allowed to drink alcohol more than a specified limit, thereby remaining on standby at all times and being alert for duty as and when they were asked to report.

Since it made sense for such an order to exist, none of the other Nazi commanders protested it and it went into effect very quickly. But Himmler did not stop his rampage there – he had Gesche followed and managed to collect evidence that the FBK commander had violated this mandate. The evidence he had, meant that Himmler was holding a card over Gesche's head – he had no choice but to sign a statement that said that he would no longer consume alcohol for the next three years.

If he did break this agreement, he would be expelled from the SS. Himmler was probably planning to get him drunk on the sly and then have him thrown out – sadly for him, that never happened.

It goes without saying that not many of the men of the SS were happy with this mandate in general. Their general discontent, going hand in hand with Hitler's fondness for Gesche, forced Himmler's hand – he had no choice but to remove the ban within a few months, thereby rendering the statement that Gesche had signed null and void.

But Himmler did not step down – he maintained a close watch on Gesche and eyed him like a hawk; the moment Gesche made a mistake, he would be ready to take him down.

And a mistake Gesche did soon make. In the early months of the year 1942, Gesche, who had gone back to drinking heavily after the ban was lifted, ended up threatening a fellow SS officer. Things became so bad that he ended up pulling a pistol on the man. This was exactly the moment that Himmler needed – as soon as he had been told of what had taken place, he made his move.

This time, not even his close relationship with Hitler could change his fate. Himmler had evidence collected against him and with all the witness reports and the data identifying Gesche as an alcoholic, it was easy to get rid of him – Gesche was removed from the command of the FBK. He was also made to sign another agreement which required him to stay away from spirits for the next three years.

With the demotion came movement across borders; Gesche was then sent to the Eastern Front to serve in the battlefield – he was placed in the Waffen-SS, 5th SS Panzer Division Wiking. These men were engaged in fighting harsh battles with none other than the Soviet Union themselves – they fought long and hard and bitterly to keep control of Caucasus, an area that was rich in oil.

It goes without saying that the side that took control of this area would be very powerful indeed; the oil meant a whole new dimension to the war, especially on the machinery and the weaponry front.

Gesche was wounded during one of the skirmishes with the Russians and ended up having to be taken away from battle. His evacuation meant that tales of his bravery spread – he had distinguished himself in combat and in Hitler's eyes, he had managed to redeem himself. Pleased with the bravery and the fighting ability he had shown in battle, Hitler had him reinstated as head of the FBK in December of the year 1942.

However, there was another, more sinister reason for Hitler to bring him back and give command of FBK to Gesche. Given the fact that these men had served him personally at his headquarters, it went without saying that they were in possession of intelligence that could very easily be used against the Furher.

Even if they were no longer part of his entourage, they knew sensitive information – if they were sent to the Eastern Front and by chance, if they were captured, then the Soviets could end up torturing them for information which they would have no choice but to reveal.

In fear for his own life and to make sure his power was not threatened, Hitler not only reinstated Gesche, but he also ordered that any man who had worked at his headquarters would not be sent to the Eastern Front – he wanted to keep all the secrets of Nazi Germany safe and contained in Nazi hands only.

It was in the month of December of the year 1944 that Gesche's time would end in the FBK. Once again, he shot himself in his own foot, just like his predecessor had done. Like Gildisch, Gesche also gave in to the bottle – he became utterly drunk and intoxicated, to the point that he ended up not only whipping his pistol out at a comrade, but also firing shots at him. Himmler, still irate and still waiting for an opportunity to pounce on Gesche, had him thrown out.

And Hitler could not protest this time, since the incident showed that the soldier was incapable of controlling himself and his vice. Himmler wrote a very strong letter to Gesche, who was not only thrown out of the FBK but demoted very badly.

He said that he could not tolerate drunkards, especially not within the Furherkorps and was therefore, demoting the man. It was only his long relationship with the SS – since he was one of the oldest Nazis to exist – that he was being allowed to remain in the SS.

Himmler also said that he would give Gesche another opportunity to, *"... serve in the Dirlewanger Brigade..."* and that if he proved himself in battle once again, in front of the enemy, he could wipe away the shame that had collected upon his being from his nasty behavior.

Himmler added that he was expecting Gesche to never again touch alcohol – the solider was to abstain for the rest of his life, and if he could not do so, then he was expected to, *"... hand in your (Gesche's) resignation..."*

Bruno Gesche, commander of the FBK, went down from such a high position to a demotion that lasted down nine full grades. He was an SS-Obersturmbannführer who was now an SS-Unterscharführer. In his place, Franz Schadle took command of the FBK, while Gesche himself was sent to Dirlewanger, which served as the SS penal unit.

Now, a post in this unit meant no return – at that point in the war, these men were definitely not coming back and it served as the penal unit of the SS for a reason. They were on the forefront of the most dangerous battle and anyone who was not wanted as part of the general SS and were considered disposable, were sent there.

If Gesche went there, there was almost a hundred percent possibility that he would not return alive – which was Himmler's plan all along, of course. Hitler's favorite bodyguard was facing his inevitable end, and the Furher obviously did not intervene.

But even if Hitler could not say anything, other commanders and leaders did – SS-Gruppenführer Hermann Fegelein and Maximilan von Herff, who was SS-Obergruppenführer, protested.

They said that this order to send Gesche to the Eastern Front went against the orders Hitler had issued when Gesche had been reinstated – it directly went against his mandate of not deploying the men who had served at his HQ to these place to prevent the leaking of intelligence.

Given the fact that this order had come from Hitler himself, Himmler could do very little about it – Gesche was spared the Dirlewanger Brigade and thus, his life was saved.

Despite his good luck, however, Gesche would never come back to the FBK. His time there, as Hitler's personal bodyguard and friend, was done – he had caused one too many incidents and had been demoted completely. Instead, he was assigned to the 16th SS Panzergrenadier Division Reichsführer, which in the end, had no choice but to surrender to the American men in Italy in the year 1945.

The last known internment we have of Bruno Gesche is by the Western Allies on the 22nd of March 1947 – this is from the records that have been kept at Deutsche Dienststelle (WASt), which for those who don't know, is a government agency in Berlin which maintains all the records of members of all the military personnel during the war.

What happened to Gesche afterwards is not clear. He died much later in life, if sources are to be believed, in the 80s. He fell out of the public eye and retreated into his own life.

Sadly, his alcoholism seemed to have gotten the better of him – from the head of FBK, he went to being a soldier that no one even knew

CHAPTER 5

ROCHUS MISCH – TO THE VERY END

Rochus Misch is perhaps one of the most famous of Hitler's personal bodyguards, garnering huge media attention when he passed away a couple of years ago as one of the few survivors of the World War and Hitler's guards.

Born in the year 1917, on the 29th of July, Misch was part of the LSSAH which were personally responsible for the Furher's safety and defense. Wounded badly in the early stages of the Second World War, during the Polish campaign, he was sent back home to recover from his injuries, following which, he ended up being part of the FBK.

It was here that he served in various capacities in Hitler's guard – he was a bodyguard, he was courier as well as telephone operator for the dictator with whom he was personally connected.

Misch was born in the Province of Silesia, which is now known as Stare Siołkowice, located in Poland. His father was a construction worker who had also taken part in the First World War – having sustained grievous injuries, he died very quickly. Misch would soon lose both his parents; his mother died of pneumonia when he was very young and it was only his grandparents who raised him.

Tragedy continued to strike the family – Misch's elder brother, Bruno, ended up dying in a swimming accident that took place in the year 1922.

Raised by his grandparents, Misch's childhood wasn't exactly a fully happy one. His grandfather refused to let him go to school after he turned eight years old; he insisted that Misch stay at home and learn a trade. The young boy later moved to Hoyerswerda, where he apprenticed with the Schmuller and Model firm, training to be a painter.

In the year 1935, he ended up joining the Masters' School of Fine Arts in Cologne, but he could not stay there for a very long time – he went back to Hoyerswerda to continue his training.

It was around this time, in the year 1938, that he met his wife, Gerda. The two got married on New Year's Eve in 1942, soon after which Gerda gave birth to a little girl named Brigitta, who, when the war came to an end, supported Jewish causes despite her father's affiliation with the Nazi Party.

It was in the year 1937 that Misch got a call up notice to join the military service. He joined the SS- Verfügungstruppe or the SS-VT, which was the forerunner of the Waffen-SS and often called the SS-VT. He rose through the ranks very quickly and it was not long before he was picked out to be one of the twelve men who would form Hitler's personal bodyguards at the LSSAH.

When the Germans launched the Polish invasion in earnest in the month of September, in 1939, Misch was part of it. He was in the regiment that was attached to the XIII Army Corps. Given that he had quite the battle prowess, his company commander picked him to negotiate the surrender of Polish troops. This negotiation was to be held near Warsaw, close to the end of September at the Battle of Modlin.

Of course, the reason they picked him was not very grandeur as he expected – he had a small ability to converse in Polish, though he was not very good at it. But he was their only option and it was augmented by the fact that he could fight well; the negotiations were carried out but Germany could not convince the Polish to give up and thus failed. The Nazis headed back to their camp and that was when Misch was badly injured.

As they were nearing camp, about 80 meters from the fort, the enemy began to fire at them from the back. A number of these bullet rounds hit Misch, who obviously fell down and quickly blacked out.

A few of his German comrades carried him out and took him to an aid station, but his injuries were grievous and he had to be transferred to different hospitals. It took another six weeks in a convalescent home for him to fully recover.

For this service he rendered in the negotiation, Misch was given an award – he was bestowed with the Iron Cross, Second Class. He was then recommended to be part of the FBK – as we saw previously, the twelve men who were handpicked to be Hitler's closest bodyguards, were drawn from a number of organizations such as the LSSAH, SS and a number of other places.

Misch, as one of the LSSAH members, was chosen to be part of this; particularly because he could no longer go back to the front lines. In May of 1940, Misch was then transferred to the FBK, becoming a junior member of Hitler's permanent bodyguards.

As one of the men closest to Hitler, Misch traveled with him where ever he went. He performed a number of services, from being his telephone operator to being his courier to being his valet and orderlies.

As we discussed previously, as long as the FBK members were on duty, Hitler let only these men near him and they were never asked to give their weapon up. While this was comforting to the men, Misch was often worried about the fact they were armed with just Walther PPK 7.65 pistols.

In the year 1945, in January, after Germany was defeated in the Battle of the Bulge (despite causing heavy losses to the Allied side and taking them completely by surprise, rendering it one of the bloodiest battles the USA had fought in the Second World War), Misch, along with all the other men who served as Hitler's personal staff, moved into the Führerbunker and Vorbunker, both of which were located under the Reich Chancellery Garden, located in Berlin.

The then FBK commanding officer, Franz Schadle, picked Misch to be the telephone operator at the bunker, which meant that he would have to handle all the communication in and out of the place directly.

Up until the very end of the war, Misch was dedicated to this job – he didn't leave it until the war came to an end in 1945. On the 22nd of April, Schadle called him up and informed him that there were two spots on the plane that was headed out of Berlin for his wife and daughter.

Misch received a temporary reprieve from his duty and drove up to where his family was, but his wife refused to take their daughter and leave. Misch had no choice but to go back to the Reich Chancellery, wherein he learnt that the reason he was being given those spots on the plane was because Hitler was releasing all the staff to leave Berlin. The Red Army was coming in and the Germany was fast losing.

On the 30th of April, the Soviets were almost right upon the bunker – they were less than 500 meters away.

It was that very afternoon that Hitler and his wife killed themselves; it was Misch who found their bodies. He followed Heinz Linge, Hitler's chief valet and Otto Gunsche, another famous solider, to the Fuhrer's private room within the bunker.

When the door opened, Misch glanced in quickly – he reported that he saw Eva on the sofa, her legs were drawn up, as she was to Hitler's left. Her eyes were wide open, he said, and she was obviously dead.

Hitler was also definitely gone – his head had, *"...fallen forward slightly..."* Misch was about to leave to inform Schadle of the events that had taken place, but stopped to see that Hitler's body was removed from the study and then wrapped up neatly in a blanket.

A number of men came forward to pick up the corpse and Misch stood rooted to the spot as they carried it past him. He then left to tell Schadle what happened; the commander then instructed him to get back to his telephone duty.

Unterscharführer Retzbach, another one of soldiers there, asked Misch if he was going up to see what was happening, but he refused to do so. Gunsche, one of Hitler's famous soldiers, came rushing down – he knew Misch and he informed him that Hitler and Eva had both been burned in the Reich Chancellery's garden.

Misch would remain at the bunker for a while to come; he witnessed a number of things within the place following Hitler's death itself. For instance, the Propaganda Minister of Nazi Germany, a man named Joseph Goebbels, had moved into the place with his wife and six children.

Magda Goebbels is infamous for having murdered her own children – when she realized that Germany had lost the war and Hitler himself had committed suicide, she poisoned her six kids and then both she and her husband killed themselves on the 1st of May, 1945.

Misch would later admit that this act of killing their own kids was the most unsettling thing he had experienced in his career as Hitler's bodyguard. Before he killed himself, though, Joseph Goebbels released Misch from his service and told him that he was free to leave.

Misch himself, along with another mechanic by the name of Johannes Hentschel, were the only people who were left behind in the bunker – they maintained contact with their wives on the outside through letters, in case something happened to them.

It was then that Misch went up to the where Schadle was – he had to report to him one last time and then inform him that he had been released from service finally. By that time, Schadle – who had been shot in the leg – had a gangrenous injury. When Misch told him that the Goebbels had let him go from service, Schadle, who seemed to be rather fond of the man, advised him on how to escape the Soviets surrounding the area.

After he helped Misch, he shot himself and committed suicide like all the other residents of the bunker.

Just hours before the Red Army took the bunker, Misch fled the area, on the morning of 2 May. A couple of other soldiers, who were also fleeing the surrounding places, met up with him and together, they went north through the U-Bahn tunnels.

But it wasn't meant to be an escape – they were captured very shortly and taken into custody. Misch himself was taken to Moscow, where he was tortured. The Soviets wanted information about Hitler's last days and since Misch had been one of the men closest to him, he provided a veritable goldmine of information for them.

For the next eight years, Misch would be imprisoned at the Soviet forced labor camps – the leader, Joseph Stalin was worried about possible escape on Hitler's part and was extremely interested in learning about his last days.

46

Misch was finally released from his imprisonment in the year 1953 and afterwards, he returned to West Berlin. He went back to his own home, which was – actually – located quite close to the bunker itself. His wife was working as a teacher in Neukölln and they reunited.

For a man who had returned to civilian life after a lifetime at war, readjusting to life was extremely difficult – he did not know what to do now that he was out of captivity. He took up a number of odd jobs, such as being a driver and a porter – the contacts he had made during the war helped out where they could by getting him these job offers.

However, most of these jobs required that he leave Berlin, and his wife was staunchly against that idea.

In the end, he would end up starting his own business; he got a loan from some German philanthropists and bought out a small shop in Berlin. When the Americans occupied Berlin, he also ran another small business on the side, making and selling peanut butter for their troops. This business had been started by a friend of his and in fact, it became so successful that he even thought about leaving his own shop – his wife convinced him not to do so.

His wife, Gerda, had also been serving the parliament of West Berlin for a number of years; now, in 1975, she was elected to it and became part of it. Almost 15 years later, in 1998, she developed Alzheimer's and passed away quickly. Misch, on the other hand, continued to run his own shop until he retired in the year 1985.

Later in life, he would go on to publish a memoir in German, titled, 'Der letzte Zeuge', which was translated as 'The Last Witness' – the book came out in 2008 and was republished in English in the year 2014.

Rochus Misch is widely accepted to be the last surviving member of the men who had served at the bunker. Up until the very end, he apparently remained loyal to Hitler.

He would later say of Hitler that the man was not a brute or a monster like the world perceived him to be, *"…he was very normal… not like what is written… he was a wonderful boss."*

What is interesting is that Misch's wife was apparently of Jewish descent; much later, his daughter, Brigitta, came to know from her mother's mother that Gerda had had Jewish ancestry. Gerda herself refused to mention this fact and Gerda's father had turned his back on it, not acknowledging it at all. Brigitta, who had a career as an architect, ended up supporting Jewish causes.

Misch was interviewed a number of times by a French journalist named Nicolas Bourcier and wrote a biography based on his accounts, the book was published in 2006 in French and later translated to a number of other languages.

Misch, who lived in Berlin, continued to remain at the same house that he had come back to at the end of his captivity with the Soviets – he regularly received visitors who wanted to speak to him about the War and Hitler himself.

It was on the 5th of September, 2013, at the age of 96, Rochus Misch passed away. He was the last member of Hitler's personal bodyguard and had served the man faithfully, remaining utterly loyal to him until the very end.

CONCLUSION

Hitler, for all that he was hated by the world and committed innumerable atrocities, was a man of intelligence and charisma.

It comes as no surprise then, that his men were ready to follow him to the very end – people like Misch were convinced, even after the war ended, that he was not a man to be feared, but just an ordinary man who went to achieve great things.

Hitler surrounded himself with the strongest men on the planet; he was one of the few leaders in the world who had such a huge number of soldiers working in his defense. No other war leader has had such expansive protection – it isn't any surprise that the Allies could never get close to him...

Thank you for purchasing this book, I hope you found it informative!

If you enjoyed this book, do you think you could leave me a review on Amazon? Just search for this title and my name on Amazon to find it. Thank you so much, it is very much appreciated!

OTHER BOOKS WRITTEN BY ME

Below you'll find some of my other popular books that are popular on Amazon and Kindle as well. You can visit my author page on Amazon to see other work done by me. (Cyrus J. Zachary).

1. **World War 2 Women**

2. **World War 2 Women – Book 2**

3. **World War 2 Submarines**

4. **World War 2 Submarines – Book 2**

5. **Holocaust Survivor Accounts**

6. **Holocaust Survivor Accounts – Book 2**

7. **Holocaust Rescuers**

8. **Holocaust Rescuers – Book 2**

9. **Holocaust Survivors Box Set**

You can simply search for these titles on the Amazon website with my name to find them.

LIBRARY BUGS BOOKS

Like books?

Would you like them delivered to you every week?

Do you like non-fiction books on a huge range of different topics?

We send out e-books every week so we can share our books with the world!

We have books every week on AMAZON that we send to our email list.

If you want in, then visit the link below to sign up and sit back and wait for new books to be sent straight to your inbox!

It couldn't be simpler!

www.LibraryBugs.com

If you want books delivered straight to your inbox, then visit the link above and soon you'll be receiving a great list of e-books every week!

Enjoy :)

CYRUS J. ZACHARY

Cyrus is a very avid history buff but his biggest joy is the interesting history of our World War's. For the last 2 decades Cyrus has dedicated himself to continue learning and applying his knowledge to his books.

His books are written from an angle so as to give the reader maximum entertainment and information in the most effective format. Cyrus believes the more you learn the more you grow, so he always instils that in every book he writes.

Cyrus likes to call Ireland home where he spends his spare time hiking and enjoying the countryside with his family.

CPSIA information can be obtained
at www.ICGtesting.com
Printed in the USA
BVOW09s0213251117
501187BV00001B/65/P